ANIMALS WITHOUT BRAINS!

SEA STARS ARE BRAINLESS!

By Amanda Vink

Gareth Stevens
PUBLISHING

Please visit our website, www.garethstevens.com. For a free color catalog of all our high-quality books, call toll free 1-800-542-2595 or fax 1-877-542-2596.

Library of Congress Cataloging-in-Publication Data

Names: Vink, Amanda, author.
Title: Sea stars are brainless! / Amanda Vink.
Description: New York : Gareth Stevens Publishing, [2020] | Series: Animals without brains! | Includes index.
Identifiers: LCCN 2019021115| ISBN 9781538245941 (paperback) | ISBN 9781538245965 (library bound) | ISBN 9781538245958 (6 pack)
Subjects: LCSH: Starfishes–Juvenile literature.
Classification: LCC QL384.A8 V56 2020 | DDC 593.9/3–dc23
LC record available at https://lccn.loc.gov/2019021115

Published in 2020 by
Gareth Stevens Publishing
111 East 14th Street, Suite 349
New York, NY 10003

Designer: Sarah Liddell
Editor: Amanda Vink

Photo credits: Cover, p. 1 Antonio Martin/Shutterstock.com; background used throughout Sanjatosic/Shutterstock.com; p. 5 aquapix/Shutterstock.com; pp. 7, 13 Damsea/Shutterstock.com; p. 9, 11 NatureDiver/Shutterstock.com; p. 15 Auscape/Contributor/Universal Images Group/Getty Images; p. 17 Krzysztof Bargiel/Shutterstock.com; p. 19 Dan Bagur/Shutterstock.com; p. 21 Richard Whitcombe/Shutterstock.com.

Printed in the United States of America

CPSIA compliance information: Batch #CW20GS: For further information contact Gareth Stevens, New York, New York at 1-800-542-2595.

CONTENTS

Boldface words appear in the glossary.

Taking a Walk

If you've been to an aquarium or beach, it's likely that you've seen a sea star. It might surprise you that sea stars have no brains! Yet they can walk around and hunt **prey**. How do they do that?

Not a Fish!

Many people call sea stars "starfish." However, they aren't fish! Sea stars are invertebrates, a group of animals that have no backbone or **skeleton**. Over 2,000 species, or kinds, of sea stars live in the world's oceans.

Bloodless

Sea stars have a water vascular system, which means that instead of blood, seawater moves through their bodies. Water is brought into and out of their bodies through a small bony plate called a madreporite, found at the center of their body.

MADREPORITE

Many Arms

Many sea stars have five arms, but others may have up to 40 arms. If an arm is lost, it will **regenerate**! Sea stars also have simple eyes on the tip of each arm.

Skin Deep

Sea stars have radial symmetry, which means their bodies are planned around a center point. They have rough skin that **protects** them, and they come in many different colors—both to scare away and to hide from **predators**.

Out-of-Body Experience

Sea stars are **carnivores**. Many sea stars can push their **stomachs** outside of their bodies! While this may seem like a strange thing to do, it allows sea stars to eat animals that are larger than their small mouths.

An Arm Up

A sea star has a simple nervous system. This allows it to receive and respond to **information** from the world around them. Scientists believe that without a brain to handle information, the arms share knowledge. One arm can take charge of the whole creature!

Moving Along

The bottom of a sea star is covered with clear tube-like feet. These tubes help the sea star to move across surfaces and hold on to prey. The sea star can also create glue-like matter to help it stick.

A Keystone Species

Sea stars are an important predator. They are a keystone species, which means their activities affect the whole **ecosystem**. Without sea stars, the numbers of other animals would become out of balance. Sea stars don't need brains to be amazing!

GLOSSARY

carnivore: an animal that eats other animals

ecosystem: all the living things in an area

information: knowledge obtained from study or observation

predator: an animal that hunts other animals for food

prey: an animal that is hunted by other animals for food

protect: to keep safe

regenerate: to grow back

skeleton: the bony frame of the body

stomach: the body part where food goes and begins to be broken down after an animal swallows it

FOR MORE INFORMATION

BOOKS

Housel, Debra J. *Incredible Invertebrates.* Huntington Beach, California: Teacher Created Materials, 2012.

Laughlin, Kara L., *In the Deep Blue Sea: Sea Stars.* North Mankato, Minnesota: Child's World Publishing, 2017.

WEBSITES

Kids Answers
answersingenesis.org/kids/sea-animals/
This website features information and activities about sea stars and other marine life.

National Geographic Kids: Sea Star
kids.nationalgeographic.com/animals/sea-star/
Check out this website to learn more about sea stars and other animals.

Publisher's note to educators and parents: Our editors have carefully reviewed these websites to ensure that they are suitable for students. Many websites change frequently, however, and we cannot guarantee that a site's future contents will continue to meet our high standards of quality and educational value. Be advised that students should be closely supervised whenever they access the internet.

INDEX